Life is Such a GIANT Plus

(Positive thinking for kids - by a kid!)

BY BREE MACFARLANE

Dedicated to my Grandpa
and all the dreamers

© 2023. BREE MACFARLANE. ALL RIGHTS RESERVED.

This book is all about ME

MY NAME _____

MY AGE _____

Fave Person _____

Fave Food _____

Fave Animal _____

Fave Activity _____

SING A SONG

You can sing a song before you sleep or whenever you please.

It's a great idea to share your favorite tune with your parent or or caregiver.

Additionally, you can create a song on your own, perhaps about your beloved pet or how today will be the most exceptional day of the week.

Ensure that it's a joyous and uplifting melody!

THE BLUES

Did you know that African-American people invented a type of music called "The Blues"? They're songs that sound really sad and slow. Sometimes you might feel sad or lonely too, and that's okay.

But as soon as you start feeling that way, try to do something that makes you happy! You can suggest going on an outing with your mum or dad or caregiver, or read your favourite book. You can even do some gardening and pick some weeds or tidy up your room.

It doesn't matter what you do, as long as it makes you feel better! So if you ever have a bad case of "The Blues", just jump up and do something fun to make those sad feelings go away!

FROM A SEA OF SADNESS MY SHINY SEAPLANE SOARS UP TOWARDS THE SUNSHINE...

IMAGINATION...

Imagine something really cool, like a superhero flying through the sky or a mermaid swimming in the ocean. You can also imagine something you love, like your pet dog or cat, or a special place like a park or a beach.

When you use your imagination, you can create anything you want in your mind and it can be really fun!

FAIRNESS

Hey, sometimes things don't go the way we want them to, and that's not always fair.

Bad things can happen, but it's okay because we can deal with them! Even though it can be tough, remember that you don't have to do it all on your own.

You can ask for help from people you trust like your mum or dad, caregiver, friends, or teachers. There's lots of help available if you just ask for it.

So, if something doesn't seem fair, remember that it's okay to ask for help and support. You've got this!

MIND/BRAIN THINKING PICTURE

Imagine your brain is like a big picture book that helps you think. It's important to look at the pictures and think before you do anything, because sometimes we might do something we wish we hadn't.

So, always remember to use your brain and think before you act!

SUNNY SIDE UP

Have you ever heard the song "Always Look on the Bright Side of Life"? It's a really fun and catchy song!

If you sing it when you're feeling sad or down, it can make you feel better and even bring a smile to your face!

I like to call it "putting the Sunny Side Up". It means trying to focus on happy thoughts, even when things aren't going well.

One way to practice feeling happy is to stand in front of a mirror and say "Cheese!" while practicing your smile.

Your smile is one of the best things you have, so keep on smiling and looking on the bright side of life!

CA$H FOR KIDS

Maybe, if you want something, ask your caregiver or Mum or Dad if they need something done - so you can earn some cash.

Earn your own money!

Its heaps cooler!

WIN-WIN SITUATIONS

When you're making a deal with your mum or dad, it's important to be fair and use your head. Don't just demand things – try to find a compromise that works for both of you.

For example, if you want something, like more TV time, you could offer to clean your room in exchange. That way, you get what you want and your mum, dad or caregiver gets something they want too!

WIN-WIN SITUATIONS CONTINUED...

It's also a good idea to let others win sometimes. For example, if you're playing a game with a younger person, you could let them win to give them a bit of fun and encouragement.

Remember, making a good deal is like shaking hands – both people should be happy with the agreement. So always try to find a solution that works for everyone involved!

Do you like the sea? I love to play safely around water.

Do you like to swim?

FAV COLOURS

What colour makes you feel the happiest?

There are so many colours, millions of them! Think about it and choose the colour that brings a smile to your face.

My favourite happy colour is royal blue, what's yours?

ITS OK TO DREAM!

Fairy Park is a really special place that I love to visit. It's located near Anakie in Victoria, Australia.
At Fairy Park, you can see lots of scenes from your favorite fairy tales! And there's music and movement to make it even more magical. You can even explore waterfalls!

But the most fun part is Camelot Playground. It has lots of cool things to play on like slides, swings, and tunnels to crawl through.

Remember, it's okay to dream and imagine magical worlds like the ones you see at Fairy Park. So next time you visit, let your imagination run wild and have fun!

LOVE IS SPECIAL

I REALLY LOVE MY MUM AND DAD, MY UNCLES, AND MY FRIENDS SO MUCH!

I ALSO HAVE A SUPER COOL AUNT WHO IS YOUNGER THAN ME. AND, GUESS WHAT? I'M SO LUCKY TO HAVE A GREAT GRANNY WHOM I LOVE A LOT!

DID YOU KNOW THAT SOME PEOPLE HAVE TWO MUMS OR TWO DADS, OR CAREGIVERS WHO LOVE AND PROTECT THEM JUST AS MUCH?

WHO ARE THE SPECIAL PEOPLE IN YOUR LIFE THAT YOU LOVE AND CARE ABOUT?

POSITIVITY IS GOOD

Sometimes we feel unhappy even when everything is okay. It's like a cloud of sadness that comes and covers our heart. But we can make the cloud go away by saying nice things to ourselves.

One way is to look in the mirror and say, "I am happy and everything is wonderful" five times. It might sound silly, but it helps us feel happier.

So, next time you feel sad, try saying nice things to yourself and see how you start feeling better. And if you want to make yourself smile, you can say something like, "I am awesome" or "I can do anything I want".

LAUGH A LOT!

At least once a day have a good laugh!

Make up a joke to share with your Mum or Dad or Caregiver, or your friends.

Make up a funny play! And get your whole family to watch.

Remember: Lots of laughs = lots of smiles!

HAVING FUN

Wow, there are so many ways to have fun and enjoy yourself!

You can have fun by going to the movies or watching your favourite TV show. But did you know that you can also create your own fun?

You can make up your own games or quizzes. You could even dress up as a silly clown! And if you love reading, you could go to the library and find an exciting book to read.

There are hundreds of ways to have lots of fun, so why not try something new today?

Do you like being cold?
BRRRRRR!!!

These beautiful colours are called an AURORA.

BE KIND TO OTHERS

Think about others. If you see someone hurt try to help. If you see someone being bullied tell a teacher or your Mum or Dad or Caregiver. Being kind means you care about other people and think about how they feel. When you're kind to others, it makes you feel good too!

So always try to be thoughtful and caring towards others.

HAPPINESS

What is Happiness?

Happiness is feeling really good inside! It's like when you wake up in the morning and you're excited for the day ahead.

It's when you smile really big because something makes you really happy. It's when you feel like everything is just super awesome!

Happiness is when you make someone happy. My Grandpa always says to me:

"You make me happy"!

...and remember you are always loved, no matter what!

THE END

(now see if you can find the animal on every page,
but look carefully, there even might be two!)

www.ingramcontent.com/pod-product-compliance
Lightning Source LLC
Chambersburg PA
CBHW041202290426
44109CB00002B/102